Property Of
████████

OUR CHANGING EARTH

W9-DJI-489

THE ATMOSPHERE

Jason D. Nemeth

PowerKiDS press

New York

Published in 2012 by The Rosen Publishing Group, Inc.
29 East 21st Street, New York, NY 10010

Copyright © 2012 by The Rosen Publishing Group, Inc.

All rights reserved. No part of this book may be reproduced in any form without permission in writing from the publisher, except by a reviewer.

First Edition

Editor: Amelie von Zumbusch
Book Design: Greg Tucker

Photo Credits: Cover, pp. 8, 12, 17 Shutterstock.com; p. 4 Photodisc/Valueline/Thinkstock; pp. 5, 16, 22 Jupiterimages/Creatas/Thinkstock; p. 6 © www.iStockphoto.com/Jeremy Mayes; pp. 7 (top), 19 Hemera/Thinkstock; p. 7 (bottom) T. H. Klimmeck/Shutterstock.com; p. 9 Ammit/Shutterstock.com; p. 10 Digital Vision/Thinkstock; p. 11 Medioimages/Photodisc/Thinkstock; p. 13 Space Frontiers/Getty Images; p. 14 NASA via Getty Images; p. 15 Pat Gaines/Getty Images; p. 18 Ryan McVay/Photodisc/Thinkstock; p. 20 Michael Blann/Lifesize/Thinkstock; p. 21 David McNew/Getty Images.

Library of Congress Cataloging-in-Publication Data

Nemeth, Jason D.
 The atmosphere / by Jason D. Nemeth. — 1st ed.
    p. cm. — (Our changing earth)
 Includes index.
 ISBN 978-1-4488-6170-5 (library binding) — ISBN 978-1-4488-6298-6 (pbk.) — ISBN 978-1-4488-6299-3 (6-pack)
 1. Atmosphere—Juvenile literature. I. Title.
 QC863.5.N45 2012
 551.5—dc23

                                        2011026166

Manufactured in the United States of America

CPSIA Compliance Information: Batch #WW12PK: For Further Information contact Rosen Publishing, New York, New York at 1-800-237-9932

CONTENTS

EARTH'S BLANKET

Without the atmosphere, Earth would be a big, frozen rock. The atmosphere is all the air that surrounds our planet. It warms Earth by trapping heat from the Sun. It also keeps us safe by blocking harmful rays and **particles** from space.

People cannot live without oxygen. When people dive deep underwater, they have to carry tanks of oxygen from which they breathe.

Earth's atmosphere makes the planet a pleasant place for people to live. Without the atmosphere, we could not live on Earth!

The atmosphere is a mix of different gases. **Oxygen** and **nitrogen** make up most of it. Oxygen is a gas that people and other animals breathe. We need it to live. Nitrogen helps things grow. However, living things cannot take in nitrogen directly from air. Plants take in nitrogen that is found in the soil. Animals get nitrogen from their food.

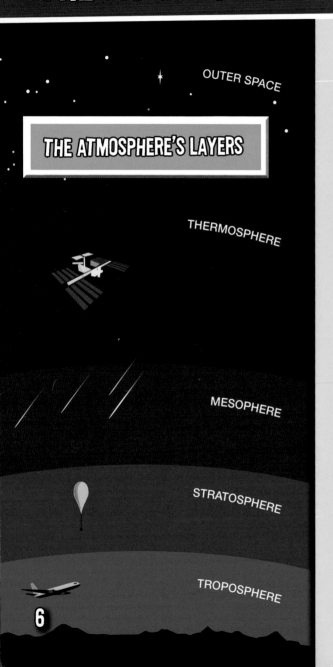

THE ATMOSPHERE'S LAYERS

OUTER SPACE

THERMOSPHERE

MESOPHERE

STRATOSPHERE

TROPOSPHERE

Earth's atmosphere has four layers. Most of our air is in the first two layers. The **troposphere** is the layer closest to Earth's surface. It reaches about 10 miles (16 km) high. The troposphere is where weather happens. Next is the **stratosphere**. It reaches up 30 miles (48 km) high.

Beyond the stratosphere is the **mesosphere**. It reaches up to about 50 miles (80 km) above Earth. The final layer is the **thermosphere**. It is the largest and reaches nearly 400 miles (644 km) high. After the thermosphere is outer space, where there is almost no air at all.

TOP: Auroras are colored lights that appear in the sky in the northern and southern parts of Earth. They are caused by particles in the thermosphere. RIGHT: Almost all airplanes stay within Earth's troposphere when they fly.

Earth's first atmosphere was likely made of hydrogen and helium. These are the universe's most common elements. Elements are the kinds of things from which all other things are made. Helium and hydrogen are very light, so they escaped into space.

Earth's **volcanoes** helped form the planet's next atmosphere. They spewed out gases such as water vapor, **carbon dioxide**, and nitrogen.

All plants make oxygen. Earth's first plants appeared over 400 million years ago.

Over time, the water vapor fell as rain. It formed Earth's oceans. Much of the carbon dioxide became buried in the oceans and soil. In time, plants appeared. They made oxygen and sent it into the air. The nitrogen and oxygen mixed to form the atmosphere we have today.

Volcanoes still let out gases into the atmosphere to this day. This volcano is Tungurahua. It is in Ecuador.

The weather on Earth happens in the troposphere. When the Sun's light reaches Earth's surface, it warms the air there. This warm air rises. The moving air creates wind. When the warm air hits colder air higher up in the troposphere, clouds form.

Different types of clouds form at different heights. Cirrus clouds are good-weather clouds. They are thin and form around 4 miles (6 km) above Earth.

Cloud-to-ground lightning, such as that shown here, takes place in the troposphere. Lightning is a flash of electricity that appears as light in the sky.

Stratus clouds form much lower. They are often dark rain clouds about 1 mile (2 km) above Earth. Cumulus clouds are big and puffy. They sometimes grow very high and bring thunderstorms.

These are cumulus clouds. Cumulus clouds are often flat on the bottom and puffy on the top. Many people think that they look like puffs of cotton.

There is a very important part of the stratosphere called the ozone layer. Ozone is a gas that blocks ultraviolet light from the Sun. This kind of light is harmful to life on Earth. It is the type of light that burns your skin when you stay in the sun for too long.

The ozone layer keeps out many harmful rays. Nonetheless, it is smart to wear sunglasses and sunscreen when you spend time outside.

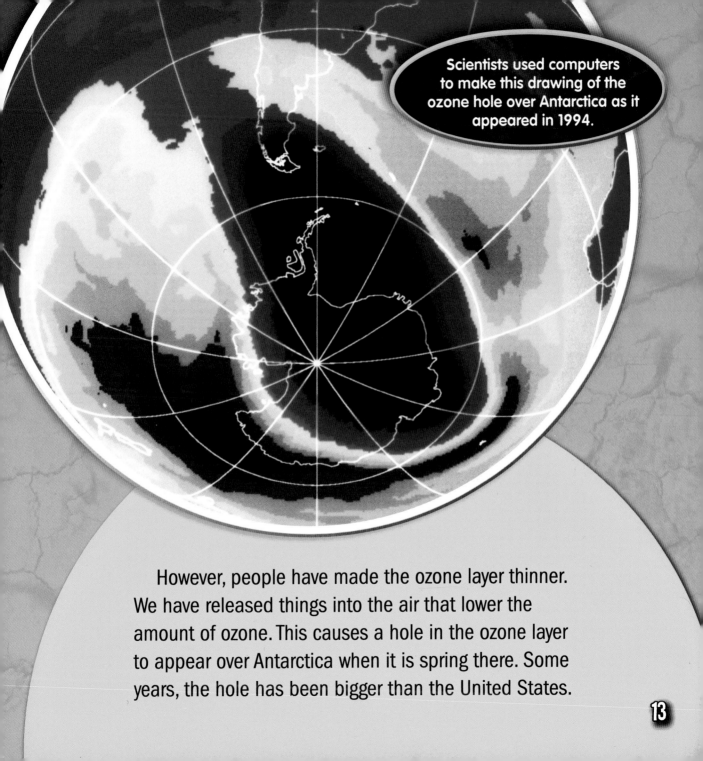

Scientists used computers to make this drawing of the ozone hole over Antarctica as it appeared in 1994.

However, people have made the ozone layer thinner. We have released things into the air that lower the amount of ozone. This causes a hole in the ozone layer to appear over Antarctica when it is spring there. Some years, the hole has been bigger than the United States.

Have you ever seen a shooting star? Shooting stars are another name for meteors. These flashes of light happen because objects from space called **meteoroids** burn as they pass through Earth's atmosphere. Most meteors happen in the mesosphere.

Here, a space shuttle is docking at the International Space Station. This is a big satellite on which scientists can stay to study space. It is in the thermosphere.

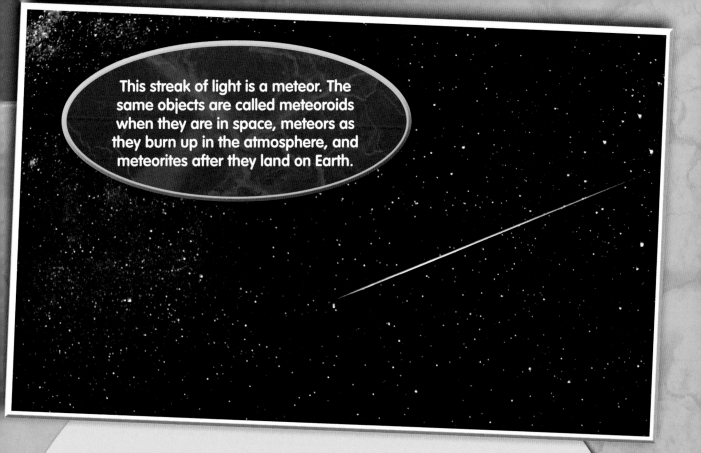

This streak of light is a meteor. The same objects are called meteoroids when they are in space, meteors as they burn up in the atmosphere, and meteorites after they land on Earth.

The farther from Earth you get, the thinner the atmosphere becomes. The particles of gas that make up the mesosphere are spaced far apart. Particles in the thermosphere are even more widely spaced.

People send spacecraft called **satellites** into the thermosphere. Satellites circle Earth. People use them to gather facts about Earth's land, weather, and more. They are even used to take pictures of Earth.

Certain gases in the atmosphere help keep Earth warm enough for life. They are called **greenhouse gases**. Examples are carbon dioxide and methane.

When the Sun shines, it warms Earth. Much of that heat gets sent back into space, though. Gases such as carbon dioxide and methane trap that heat and keep it inside Earth's atmosphere. If these gases were not there, that heat would be lost.

Greenhouse gases get their name because they trap heat inside Earth's atmosphere in the same way that glass traps heat inside a greenhouse.

Greenhouse gases keep Earth warm enough for liquid water to exist in our oceans and lakes. Liquid water is needed for life. No greenhouse gases would mean there would be only frozen water and no life on Earth.

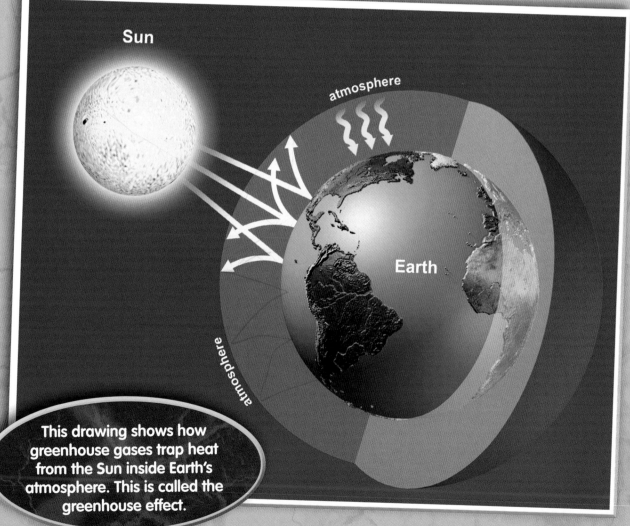

Sun

atmosphere

Earth

atmosphere

This drawing shows how greenhouse gases trap heat from the Sun inside Earth's atmosphere. This is called the greenhouse effect.

WHY IS EARTH WARMING UP?

Earth is warming up because of too many greenhouse gases. The right amount helps keep Earth warm enough for life. Too many greenhouse gases can make Earth too hot.

Americans use about 20 million barrels of oil each day. Much of this is used for gasoline.

Most of the goods we buy, such as food, clothes, and toys, are shipped by vehicles that produce greenhouse gases.

There are more greenhouse gases in the atmosphere today because of people. People burn coal and oil to make electricity and to run their cars. When these fuels burn, they release carbon dioxide into the air.

People have also cut down most of Earth's forests. Trees and other plants use carbon dioxide to grow. They take it out of the atmosphere. The fewer trees there are, the more carbon dioxide stays in the air.

Scientists use several tools to study Earth's atmosphere. They send satellites and weather balloons into the atmosphere. These have tools on them that can measure things. For example, some measure the mix of gases found at a certain level of the

Scientists use weather balloons to study the atmosphere. The balloons can rise as high as 100,000 feet (30,480 m) into the atmosphere.

atmosphere. Trackers on weather balloons are used to measure wind speed, too.

Many cities and towns have weather stations. These record daily **temperatures** and rainfall. Radar stations use radio waves to scan the atmosphere. Some scientists build computer programs to help understand how the weather works. All of these tools and more give us a picture of what the atmosphere is like.

This scientist is in a plane that has been specially set up to measure pollution in the atmosphere.

There are several ways we can help Earth's atmosphere return to normal levels of greenhouse gases. One way is by using renewable energy. Renewable energy comes from sources like the Sun and the wind. They do not produce greenhouse gases when they are used. We can also plant more trees.

The extra greenhouse gases in the atmosphere are already causing changes. For example, ice sheets at Earth's poles are melting. We will have to live with these changes even while we work to make things better.

Another thing you can do to cut down on the greenhouse gases being produced is to buy lightbulbs that use less energy.

GLOSSARY

carbon dioxide (KAHR-bun dy-OK-syd) A gas that has no smell or taste. People breathe out carbon dioxide.

greenhouse gases (GREEN-hows GAS-ez) Gases that trap heat near Earth when they are in Earth's atmosphere.

mesosphere (MEH-zuh-sfir) The layer of the atmosphere between the stratosphere and the thermosphere.

meteoroids (MEE-tee-uh-roydz) Rocks in outer space that circle the Sun.

nitrogen (NY-truh-jen) A gas without taste, color, or smell that can be found in the air.

oxygen (OK-sih-jen) A gas that has no color or taste and is necessary for people and animals to breathe.

particles (PAR-tih-kulz) Small pieces.

satellites (SA-tih-lyts) Spacecraft that circle Earth.

stratosphere (STRA-tuh-sfir) The second layer of Earth's atmosphere as you move away from Earth.

temperatures (TEM-pur-cherz) Measurements of how hot or cold things are.

thermosphere (THER-muh-sfir) The fourth layer of Earth's atmosphere.

troposphere (TROH-puh-sfeer) The layer of air that is closest to Earth's surface.

volcanoes (vol-KAY-nohz) Openings that sometimes shoots up hot, melted rock called lava.

INDEX

WEB SITES

Due to the changing nature of Internet links, PowerKids Press has developed an online list of Web sites related to the subject of this book. This site is updated regularly. Please use this link to access the list:
www.powerkidslinks.com/chng/atmos/